Fangs
CORAL SNAKES

Beware the Colors!

by Nancy White

Consultant: Raoul Bain, Biodiversity Specialist, Herpetology
Center for Biodiversity and Conservation
American Museum of Natural History
New York, New York

BEARPORT
PUBLISHING

New York, New York

Credits

Cover and Title Page, © Dennis M. Dennis; TOC, © Michael Fogden/OSF/Animals Animals/Earth Scenes; 5, © Daniel Heuclin/ NHPA/Photoshot; 6, © Maik Dobiey/Bruce Coleman; 7, © Zoltan Takacs; 8, © Sarah Meno; 9, © Larry Ditto/Bruce Coleman; 10L, © Joe McDonald/Corbis; 10R, © Jeff Hardwick; 11, © David M Dennis/OSF/Photolibrary; 12, © Jim Merli/Visuals Unlimited; 13, © Michael & Patricia Fogden/Minden Pictures/National Geographic Image Collection; 15, © Solon Morse; 16, © Susan Jennings; 17, © Robert Lubeck/Animals Animals Enterprises; 18, © Paul Freed/Animals Animals Enterprises; 19, © Paul Freed/Animals Animals Enterprises; 20, © Michael Fogden/Bruce Coleman; 21, © Michael P. Fogden/Bruce Coleman; 22L, © Michael D. Kern/ Nature Picture Library; 22R, © Robert Valentic/Nature Picture Library; 23A, © JH Pete Carmichael/Riser/Getty Images; 23B, © Maik Dobiey/Bruce Coleman; 23C, © Snowleopard1/Shutterstock; 23D, Susan Jennings; 23E, © Paul Freed/Animals Animals Enterprises; 23F, © Maria Dryfhout/Shutterstock; 23G, © Snowleopard1/Shutterstock; 23B, © Susan Flashman/Shutterstock; 24, © Zigmund Leszczynski/Animals Animals/Earth Scenes.

Publisher: Kenn Goin
Senior Editor: Lisa Wiseman
Creative Director: Spencer Brinker
Photo Researcher: Q2A Media: Farheen Aadil
Cover Design: Dawn Beard Creative

Library of Congress Cataloging-in-Publication Data

White, Nancy, 1942–
  Coral snakes : beware the colors! / by Nancy White.
    p. cm. — (Fangs)
  Includes bibliographical references and index.
  ISBN-13: 978-1-59716-763-5 (library binding)
  ISBN-10: 1-59716-763-0 (library binding)
  1. Coral snakes—literature. I. Title.
  QL666.O64W447 2009
  597.96'44—dc22

                    2008035304

For more information, write to Bearport Publishing Company, Inc., 101 Fifth Avenue, Suite 6R, New York, New York 10003. Printed in the United States of America.

10 9 8 7 6 5 4 3 2 1

Contents

Small but Deadly 4

A Beautiful Snake 6

A Killer's Colors 8

Coral Copycats 10

Tricky Defenses 12

Telling by Smelling 14

Out to Kill 16

A Fight to the Death 18

Deadly Babies 20

Fang Facts 22

Glossary 23

Index 24

Read More 24

Learn More Online 24

About the Author 24

Small but Deadly

It's early morning deep in the Florida woods. The light is dim. The air is hot and still. Beneath the dead leaves on the forest floor, a coral snake lies in wait. It has spotted its next meal—a lizard. This silent killer is only two feet (.6 m) long, but it has a poisonous weapon—one of the deadliest **venoms** in the world. Suddenly the coral snake **strikes** with lightning speed, sinking its **fangs** into its **victim**'s flesh.

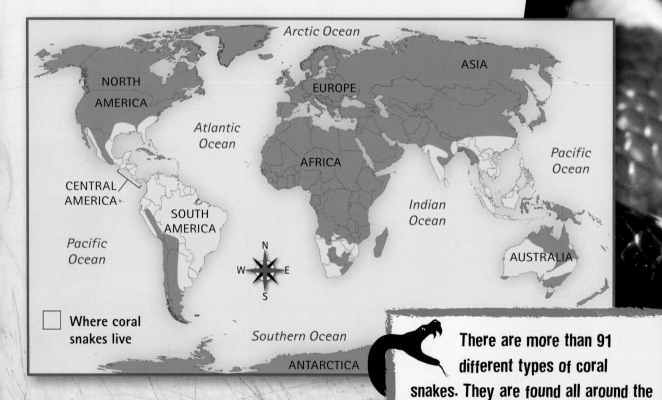

Arctic Ocean

ASIA

NORTH AMERICA

EUROPE

Atlantic Ocean

AFRICA

Pacific Ocean

CENTRAL AMERICA

SOUTH AMERICA

Indian Ocean

Pacific Ocean

AUSTRALIA

N
W　　E
S

☐ Where coral snakes live

Southern Ocean

ANTARCTICA

There are more than 91 different types of coral snakes. They are found all around the world in such places as the United States, Central America, South America, Afric, Australia, and Asia.

coral snake

A Beautiful Snake

Coral snakes are often called the most beautiful snakes in the world because of their bright colors. In North America, they have bands of red, yellow, and black that go completely around their bodies. In different parts of the world, the colors and patterns aren't always the same. In fact, some coral snakes have no banding at all.

This pretty snake isn't very big. From its narrow black head to its pointed tail, it's only 15 to 30 inches (38 to 76 cm) long—about the same length as a baseball bat. The snake's body is thin, sometimes no wider than a person's little finger.

Coral snakes **shed** their outer skin many times during their lives. Luckily, new skin grows under the old, worn-out skin. Just before the snake sheds, its bands become pale. Then the snake slithers out of the old skin, which has become white. The new skin is bright and colorful.

new skin

old skin

▲ A coral snake sheds its skin.

A Killer's Colors

The coral snake's colors aren't just pretty. They have a special meaning in nature. The colors are like a sign that says "Warning! Poison! Back off or die!" Most animals understand the warning and stay away.

Yet coral snakes do have a few enemies, such as foxes, coyotes, and larger snakes. Hawks also may try to eat coral snakes. Once a scientist in Florida found a dead hawk with a dead coral snake in its beak. Before the snake died, it had bitten and killed its attacker.

coral snake

Even with their bright colors, coral snakes are able to hide from enemies. Their small size lets them become almost invisible in tall grass or under rocks or logs.

The bright colors of this coral snake warn other animals to stay away.

Coral Copycats

Coral snakes aren't the only snakes that have colorful bands. Some harmless snakes, such as the scarlet snake and the milk snake, have them, too. Their colors make them look as though they would be venomous, even though they're not. **Predators** are often afraid to attack these "copycats" because they think they're coral snakes.

However, there are easy ways for humans to tell the difference between a real coral snake and a copycat. For example, in North America, a coral snake's red and black stripes are separated by narrow yellow bands. On a look-alike's body, the red and black stripes touch each other. Also, coral snakes have black noses, while most of the look-alikes have red noses.

▼ Milk snake

▲ Scarlet snake

In North America, some people use a rhyme to help them remember which snakes are killer corals and which ones are harmless look-alikes.

Red touching yellow,
kill a fellow.
Red touching black,
you're okay, Jack!

black nose

Tricky Defenses

A coral snake's bright colors don't always keep enemies away. Luckily, the snake has some tricky ways to defend itself. One way is to flatten itself out, making its narrow body look wider than it really is. When a predator sees this, it may back off, thinking the snake is too big to attack.

A coral snake might also **coil** its body, hide its head in the loops, and stick up its tail and wiggle it. The snake is trying to fool the enemy into thinking that its tail is actually its head. Then the snake can lift its real head and surprise the enemy with a quick bite or make a run for it.

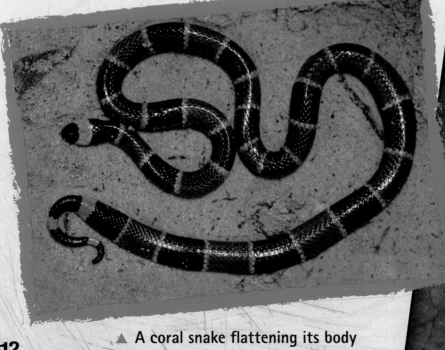

▲ A coral snake flattening its body

This coral snake from Costa Rica hides its head and wiggles its tail to fool an enemy.

Although coral snakes can bite and kill their enemies, they would rather escape than fight. Slithering down a hole made by another small animal is their favorite way to get out of danger.

Telling by Smelling

Like most snakes, coral snakes don't have very good eyesight. They can see only objects that are close up. They can't hear, either, because they have no eardrums. How, then, can they tell if an enemy is approaching—before it's too late?

A coral snake uses its nostrils and its forked tongue, which it flicks in and out, to smell. The tongue picks up any scents that are in the air. Once a coral snake smells another animal nearby, it can flatten its body, hide its head, or slither away into a deep, dark hole.

Coral snakes don't hear sounds the way humans do. Instead, they feel them. The bones in their jaws can feel the slight shaking of the ground caused by an animal or a person moving nearby.

forked tongue

Out to Kill

A coral snake usually likes to avoid other animals, but not if it's hungry. When it's ready to eat, this shy creature turns into a deadly hunter.

Night and early morning are the coral snake's favorite times to look for a meal. Flicking out its tongue, the venomous little killer slithers under rocks. It follows underground tunnels made by small animals. It sometimes pokes its tail down a hole in the ground, scaring out a small creature inside. The snake might even hide under some leaves or rocks and wait for its **prey**.

▲ Coral snakes can't open their mouths very wide.

Unlike many snakes, the coral snake's head is narrow and its jaws don't open very wide. For these reasons, it can't eat animals that are bigger than its head. So it hunts small animals such as lizards, mice, frogs, and other snakes.

lizard

A Fight to the Death

Once it finds its prey, the coral snake bites quickly. The snake's fangs are less than a quarter of an inch (6 mm) long. They're sometimes too short to break through the victim's skin. When this happens, the killer has to hold on to the struggling animal and chew in order to get its fangs into the victim's flesh.

Finally, as the venom begins to work, the prey finds itself unable to breathe or move. The coral snake can then pull the helpless victim into its mouth with its fangs and swallow it whole.

▲ A coral snake eating another snake

A coral snake attacks another snake by biting it just behind the head. This makes it hard for the other snake to bite back. Yet sometimes the coral snake does get bitten. If the other snake is venomous, then both may die.

Deadly Babies

Even baby coral snakes know all the tricky ways to hunt, kill, and defend themselves. That's a good thing because their mothers don't take care of them at all. A female coral snake usually lays about 2 to 15 eggs. Then she leaves the eggs and never comes back!

When the eggs hatch, each baby snake is only seven or eight inches (18 or 20 cm) long. They're already venomous, but their colors are pale. After about three weeks, the young snakes will shed their first skin. The colors on their new skin will be a bright warning for enemies that says "Stay away!"

▲ A baby coral snake hatching

Some animals like to eat the eggs of snakes. Female coral snakes lay their eggs in places where they will be hard to find—in rotten logs, under rocks, or in holes in the ground.

Fang Facts

- Coral snakes are related to cobras and death adders. These types of venomous snakes have two hollow fangs attached to their top jaw. When the snake bites, the venom flows through the hollow fangs into the victim.

King cobra

Death adder

- Drop for drop, a coral snake's venom is stronger and deadlier than the venom of most other snakes. It's even twice as powerful as a rattlesnake's venom. However, the coral snake can't make a lot of the poison because of its small size.

- Coral snakes don't waste their poison. To kill a small animal, such as a baby mouse, they use just a little bit of venom. They use more poison for larger animals.

Glossary

coil
(KOIL) to wind around and around in loops

shed
(SHED) to lose a layer of skin

fangs
(FANGZ) long pointy teeth

strikes
(STRIKES) attacks something

predators
(PRED-uh-turz) animals that hunt and kill other animals for food

venoms
(VEN-uhmz) poisons made by some snakes

prey
(PRAY) animals that are hunted and eaten by other animals

victim
(VIK-tuhm) an animal that is attacked or killed by another animal

Index

babies 20
colors 6, 8, 10–11, 12, 20
defense 12–13, 20
eggs 20–21
enemies 12–13, 14, 20
fangs 4, 18, 22
habitat 4

head 6, 12–13, 14, 16, 18
hunting 16–17, 20
jaws 14, 16, 22
killing 4, 8, 11, 13, 16, 18, 20, 22
look-alikes 10–11
nose 10–11, 14

prey 4, 16, 18, 22
senses 14–15
shedding 6, 20
size 4, 6, 8, 20, 22
tail 6, 12–13, 16
tongue 14–15, 16
venom 4, 10, 16, 20, 22

Read More

George, Linda. *Coral Snakes.* Mankato, MN: Capstone Press (1998).

Klein, Adam G. *Coral Snakes.* Edina, MN: ABDO Publishing Company (2006).

O'Hare, Ted. *Coral Snakes.* Vero Beach, FL: Rourke Publishing (2005).

Learn More Online

To learn more about coral snakes, visit
www.bearportpublishing.com/Fangs

About the Author

Nancy White has written many science and nature books for children. She lives in New York's Hudson River Valley.

3 1170 00801 2373